HAL•LEONARD
INSTRUMENTAL PLAY-ALONG

AUDIO ACCESS INCLUDED

PLAYBACK+
Speed • Pitch • Balance • Loop

TENOR SAX

Disney

Beauty and the Beast

T0077051

To access audio visit:
www.halleonard.com/mylibrary

Enter Code
5781-1564-2693-8333

ISBN 978-1-4950-9612-9

Wonderland Music Company, Inc.
Walt Disney Music Company

DISTRIBUTED BY

HAL•LEONARD®

7777 W. BLUEMOUND RD. P.O. BOX 13819 MILWAUKEE, WI 53213

In Australia Contact:
Hal Leonard Australia Pty. Ltd.
4 Lentara Court
Cheltenham, Victoria, 3192 Australia
Email: ausadmin@halleonard.com.au

Visit Hal Leonard Online at
www.halleonard.com

ARIA

TENOR SAX

Music by ALAN MENKEN
Lyrics by TIM RICE

BE OUR GUEST

TENOR SAX

Music by ALAN MENKEN
Lyrics by HOWARD ASHMAN

BEAUTY AND THE BEAST

TENOR SAX

Music by ALAN MENKEN
Lyrics by HOWARD ASHMAN

BELLE

TENOR SAX

Music by ALAN MENKEN
Lyrics by HOWARD ASHMAN

DAYS IN THE SUN

TENOR SAX

Music by ALAN MENKEN
Lyrics by TIM RICE

EVERMORE

TENOR SAX

Music by ALAN MENKEN
Lyrics by TIM RICE

Sturdy Ballad

GASTON

TENOR SAX

Music by ALAN MENKEN
Lyrics by HOWARD ASHMAN

11

HOW DOES A MOMENT LAST FOREVER

TENOR SAX

Music by ALAN MENKEN
Lyrics by TIM RICE

THE MOB SONG

TENOR SAX

Music by ALAN MENKEN
Lyrics by HOWARD ASHMAN

SOMETHING THERE

TENOR SAX

Music by ALAN MENKEN
Lyrics by HOWARD ASHMAN